Change is ine[illegible] ... every obstacle presents an opportunity to grow and change your current conditions.

MW01659858

It's Not a Secret, It's Just Life!!!

By

Dr. D.F. Arnold

The Pocket Book That Makes Sense

Bookstand Publishing

Published by
Bookstand Publishing
Gilroy, CA

2911_5

ISBN 978-1-58909-618-9

Printed in the United States of America

U.S.A. $15.95

Canada $24.99

It's Not a Secret, It's Just Life

This powerful life changing book reveals the power that words can and will play in your life. It's full of real life stories that show the truth about the power of words we speak and allow to be spoken to us. Your attitude, mood and feelings will play a crucial part in how fulfilling your life will be. Emotions, like a common cold, get passed from person to person everyday. So when the people around you are sick with negativity, fear, and worry, be ready to catch what they have if you continue to hang around them. And since change is inevitable, you must choose to change your attitude, mood, and feelings in order to begin healing your mind and expectations of yourself. You are capable of rising to the level of expectations you place on yourself.

During this journey, what will your mood, feelings and attitude be? Will you use this new energy to continue worrying or to achieve the life you truly deserve? Either way, you will get what you focus on, so remember...***It's not a Secret, it's just Life.***

Contents

LIFE LESSONS

LIFE

I

Are You Sick & Tired?

After traveling around the country and reading books on leadership, goal setting and many other subjects, I've often found that most of the things I read were things I already knew. It is my hope you will take the concepts in this book and like me, use them as confirmation of things you already know. These applied concepts will change your mood, feelings and attitude so you are able to have a LIFE that is full of what you desire and dream about.

It is my hope that while reading this book you will not only have that "aha" moment, but you take these ideas and say, "Hey! I know that already, he's not saying anything new." The realization that you already know everything in this book is a positive one; it proves the validity of these ideas.

I want you to take what you're reading and use the content more frequently. Every second of your life your mind is working and thinking; take full advantage of its great creative power. This book will teach you how to use this power of positive thinking more often, and how to make it work for you on a more consistent basis.

In 2007 a great deal of conversation developed as a result of a new movement called "The Secret," written by Rhonda Byrne. The Secret is said to have been practiced by great men and women of the past and present, then hidden from people who refuse to believe in this great power of the mind. I have come to understand this concept differently; having realized that it isn't a secret at all...it's just LIFE.

It is all about your mood and how you operate when you're feeling certain emotions. If you're mad at someone, does it show on your face, in your attitude, or in your actions? Are you the type of person that can't wait to tell people you were treated unfairly when someone swooped in front of you and took a parking spot you had been waiting for? Or are you still angry at that "friend" who decided to date the person you recently broke up with, even though you know the person isn't right for you?

Let's address the "parking space" scenario first. To keep yourself from getting angry at the person's rude act, focus on something else. Tell yourself people come and go from the mall frequently. Parking spaces will open up soon with a little patience. You are definitely not the only person who experiences situations like these. The key is how you choose to handle them.

When this happens to me, I think of various causes for this person's behavior; maybe all the handicap spots were full and they were forced to park in this space because it's the closest and this person needs special accommodations. Maybe they didn't see me, or maybe the person is elderly and needed that space more than me. After thinking about these possible explanations, I start to feel better—my mood, feelings and attitude begin to positively change. That is, until I see them walking and they appear fine, looking to be around 20. I then take a deep breath and focus on myself and how I will choose to react. I want you to learn the power of taking your focus off of others, and the ability to focus more on your interaction and reaction to situations like these. We cannot control someone else's action, but we can control how we choose to respond.

Now what about that friend who is now dating your ex? I know, I know, you loved them. But let's be honest, think back and remember all those things that weren't right about the relationship you had with them. Now that friend will have to deal with it. Wait a minute; doesn't that make you want to pray for them☺? Once again it's not about them, your ex or your friend; it's about how you deal with what has happened. It's about you. It may be an unwritten rule that friends don't date the ex, I know it, you know it, but maybe your friend doesn't. Think how this might play out in a Hollywood movie, where you would find someone who stretches you to become the person you were destined to be. The only reason why it was possible for you to find this person was because you left an uncomfortable relationship that you made comfortable for years. What about your friend? If this were a true friend they would have asked you if it was okay, and not dated them behind your back.

One of the lessons addressed in this book is about "friendship" and the realization that everyone is not your friend and will not necessarily have your best interest in mind.

So since this has happened to you, what type of mood are you offering, negative or positive? We can feel each other's moods, so when you're sad, lonely, angry, or maybe even second guessing yourself about a decision you've made, your mood is being affected. This book will also address the adverse affect negative emotions and feelings will play in your life.

LIFE TIP: Failure like Success is a choice, and they both require effort.

2

Is it Time to Try Change?

Let's talk about positive moods. This is when you're happy or smiling, in a loving relationship, or anytime things are going good. This is when everything is going right for you. You're putting out or radiating a positive mood. At every moment in your LIFE, every hour, minute, or second, your moods and feelings are shaping the direction in which your LIFE will go.

Your goal is to make LIFE work for you. LIFE is always checking to see what type of mood, feelings, or attitude you're having at any particular moment. If you work on changing these things, you can change the direction your LIFE will go. This is similar to how satellite television works. Every so often the main satellite millions of miles away in earth's atmosphere will do a systems check to update the box to more current programming. It checks the receiver, to see if it has any usage on it that would need to be transmitted to the main office to charge you accordingly (i.e., if you ordered any pay per view movies or a fight).

When LIFE is checking the box, which is you, it's the same concept.

Let's apply this to your LIFE. You can be at work, in the shower or washing dishes. While doing your daily mundane tasks the satellite has the ability to check your receiver for any mood changes. This is how LIFE works; it's constantly checking to see what your mood, feelings or attitudes are to give you more of what you are feeling and emitting. Regardless if it's negative or positive, LIFE will continue to align you with the consequences of your actions and reactions.

There is someone who is in my life only because he is starting to realize some things. He has begun to recognize that he is not good at being a criminal, because he continues to get caught and get into trouble. He now realizes that he will need to change some things or suffer what LIFE continues to give him, which is disappointment.

Before I met him, he would do all sorts of things wrong and would always wonder why his outcome would consistently be the same. When we met for the first time, we sat and had a conversation. He began to tell me about the trouble he had been in and how it seemed as though "trouble" seemed to follow him. After listening and allowing him to vent, I said to him, trying not to be cynical or sarcastic (but believe me it was hard), "As you've been explaining all this to me, I watched this 'friend' of yours you called "trouble" get up, get a glass of water, ask me if I needed anything, to which I responded "no thanks", "trouble" then sat right back next to you, and continue to listen to the story you are telling me."

My friend looked at me with a look of confusion. I simply explained to him how LIFE has this way of making us go through things time and time again until we get it right. So if you have done something outside of the way it should have been done, you will be tested again by LIFE to see if you will continue to do things the same way, so you can receive the same outcome, or a different way in order to receive a different outcome. LIFE is always checking our mood, feelings and attitude, to give us more of what we are requesting. So if you were able to get away with something you knew was wrong but received a rush from doing it, LIFE doesn't know whether you should or shouldn't be doing it. LIFE will continue to give you what you received the joy from. It's the action performed that will give you the negative consequence, not LIFE. LIFE is just reacting to your mood, feelings, or attitude.

"The first time you performed an illegal activity how did you feel, I mean, how did you really feel?" I asked him.

"Good."

"Okay, so when the opportunity arose to do another illegal activity how did you feel this time?"

"Okay, since it wasn't that hard the first time."

"That's what I figured"

He looked at me again, with the same confused look. I explained it was easy to feel good about it, because there were no negative consequences from it yet. LIFE was saying *oh, he enjoys this activity, so I will give him more because his mood, feeling, and attitude is saying this is a good thing.*

"Now after you got caught how did you feel?" I asked.

"Confused and scared."

I asked him, if that feeling went away anytime soon?

He said, no.

That's because now LIFE is giving you more of that feeling. Now LIFE is saying, "*He is feeling scared, worried, and angry; I must give him more of that!*" Since LIFE is obedient that is what you are receiving.

"Now that you have stopped participating in illegal activities and have begun taking responsibility for your previous actions, what is happening?" I asked.

"Things are getting better, not great but better."

"Are you in a better situation doing positive things or the things that you were doing in your past?"

"The positive things."

He wanted to know when this experience would be over and I explained to him that when we make bad choices we dig ourselves into a hole. Depending on how bad the choices are will determinate how deep the hole is and how long it will take to climb out of it. But the first step is to change our mood, feelings and attitude and to begin believing that changing old habits will produce new results. Change happens when we begin changing these behaviors and start believing change is possible, and that it will happen for us regardless how deep the hole we dug ourself in.

One of the greatest things about LIFE is the short memory it has. You could've been doing something negative or unproductive for years, but the moment you decide to change your attitude, mood or feelings about it is when you can be released and begin to move in a different direction. LIFE works instantly, the moment you begin to change is the moment your LIFE begins to change.

When you begin to offer a positive mood, feeling, or attitude, you will notice that things will begin to change for you. It will begin to affect your everyday actions. For example, you do great on that project. You go to a party or a club and all eyes seem to be looking at you. While shopping you find deals on things you have been wanting. You will notice everything will begin to go your way. At that very moment LIFE is checking your mood, feelings and attitude to see if you are offering positive vibes. As you continue to have great things happen around you and to you, you begin thinking, *I'm in a zone, I'm hot right now. I'm the man, or I'm the woman.* Your mood, feelings and attitudes are offering LIFE, happiness, contentment, and joy.

It's like the basketball player who is in a zone. Many sports psychologists call this flow, meaning they can't miss a shot and everything is falling for them. Since LIFE is constantly checking to see what our mood, feelings, and attitude are we want to be more deliberate of how we are feeling every day, hour, minute, and second. LIFE is obedient to our desires and it doesn't know if we really want something or if we are just joking about it with our friends.

One of the most powerful attributes in children is their ability to dream and imagine the things they want to have and the person they want to be. They have the ability to imagine or picture themselves doing or having something they may have seen driving down the street, in a commercial or at the store. As a child we all had this ability, it wasn't until we started associating with nonbelieving adults that this ability began to dissipate from our LIFE.

I remember sitting on the porch as a child and when a car would drive down the street my friends and I would say, "That's my car." For that day we would picture ourselves driving that car, pulling up to our big houses. I distinctly remember my cousin Eric and I going to a popular store at the mall looking at riding lawnmowers. I was infatuated with them. Maybe it was because I would watch my grandfather cut our small lot on the weekends using a push mower. I knew others had acres of land that would require them to have one of these mowers to cut their grass. So to see this machine you could drive like a car and cut your grass was incredible to me.

I also remember, every weekend while in college I would wake up and take tours of model homes. I always loved the way they looked and the way they would be staged. I would think to myself, *Wow, people actually build their own houses just the way they dream of them.* Afterwards I would leave and head straight to the Mercedes Benz dealer. It had gotten to the point where the salesmen even knew me by name. You see a lot of my weekends were spent imagining what LIFE could be, but I would take it a step further. I would go visit the places that showed me what I desired. I started to think and believe that if others could do it or have it, WHY COULDN'T I!

This book isn't to brag about me or what LIFE has given to me. LIFE has brought me all of the things I imagined back then and continues to bring me more of what I dream of and desire when mood, feelings and attitude is in line. For that reason you want to be careful about what and who you listen to, what you watch, and who you hang around because some people will steal your dreams. This happens both intentionally and unintentionally. You also must be careful with the words you speak to yourself. There are certain words that can stop your imagination from working and your dreams from coming into fruition. There are plenty of words that contribute to this, but one word in particular is forbidden in my household, and that word is CAN'T. Henry Ford once said, "If you think you can or you think you can't, you're right." It's a word we all use or have used, but you need to understand the power in this word. This is one of the biggest dream killers. It will suck any form of LIFE from you. It will prevent you from pursuing everything you have ever dreamed of having. This word stops your brain from having to work if it is repeated enough. Can you recall when you were told by someone you could not do something? Consider how that one word may have changed your entire life.

It reminds me of the story of how elephants are trained. When an elephant is a baby, a trainer will tie a collar around it's neck, attach it to a chain and hammer it down to a stake in the ground. Every day the baby elephant will attempt to break the chain, believing the chain cannot hold it back. I can also imagine that day after day other elephants, older elephants that have been conditioned to stand in place and to only go as far as the chain allowed them to do so, probably saying, "Would you look at him? Every day that baby elephant thinks that he will break that chain, doesn't he know it is impossible, doesn't he know he can't?" The other elephant probably agrees and says, "Yeah, you would think he would be tired by now. Doesn't he realize that he will never break loose?" Day after day the baby elephant continues to try and break the chain, refusing to listen to what the other animals where saying. Then one day doubt began to set in, and the baby elephant begins to think that maybe the other elephants were right. Maybe he can't break through the chains. Days go by, and then months, then years and the now grown elephant won't even attempt to break the chains any more. As the years went by, the elephant only went as far as the chain would allow. It now believed that it couldn't break the chain. The trainer went back to the elephant and took the stake from the ground, and the chain from around the elephant's neck and the elephant, even though he was no longer chained, never moved from that spot. He allowed the word CAN'T to paralyze him and stop him from moving into his purpose.

LIFE TIP: One of the greatest things about LIFE is the short memory it has. You could've been doing something negative or unproductive for years, but the moment you begin to change is the moment your LIFE begins to change.

CAN'T

3

Can't

How can you dream big if you allow the word CAN'T to exist in your vocabulary? How can you dream big if you have people around you telling you what you can or cannot do? How can you dream big when you surround yourself with negative things and naysayers?

When Michael Jordon was cut from the basketball team, I wonder if he told himself he couldn't be the greatest person to ever play the game of basketball? When Bill Gates dropped out of college I wonder if he told himself this thing called Microsoft couldn't work? When Donald Trump went bankrupt, was he thinking he couldn't make it in real estate? Growing up poor, did Oprah tell herself she couldn't be one of the most influential media personalities in the world? Did Obama tell himself that because he was black and raised in a single parent home he couldn't be president? I would bet they didn't tell themselves that, but I bet others around them did. Although they may have doubted themselves, they understood the burning desire inside to be great would lead them to be successful. We all have doubts, but we must allow our passion to overpower our doubts. Understand that it will be a journey, which will start with a single step.

Remember LIFE doesn't know whether you really want something or you're faking. Whatever is happening in your LIFE at this very moment is an indication of what your mood, feeling and attitude is right now. So if you're wondering what LIFE is giving you right now, make a list of what you have and it will match up perfectly with what you are focusing on. When you use the word CAN'T, that is what your brain is focusing on, so you will receive the results of that word.

As a student advisor, when student-athletes come into my office and start to brag about the grades they are receiving in their classes, they have a positive mood, an attitude that emanates through them. There are others that come into my office and talk about how they can't stand school or their professors. When I ask them about their grades and if they are getting tutoring their response is they don't need tutoring and everything will be fine. At the end of the semester when I'm going through the grades, I pretty much know who will be successful and who won't. I often hear those same students who won't spend the time to get help, bragging about how good they are at Madden and NBA Live video games. Remember LIFE is obedient and follows whatever you are giving your attention to; whether it's studying for exams, being good to others so LIFE will be good to you, or playing video games. LIFE will work with you to make sure you get what you put your time and effort into.

Remember whenever you use the word CAN'T you just gave your mind permission to stop working. Start noticing how often you say the word CAN'T and start observing how often others use that word. Then observe what they have or what they do. Are they dreamers who are putting forth the effort to make things happen in their LIFE? Every time the word CAN'T comes out of your mouth, start thinking about what you can do and how you can make it happen. Think of it this way, if CAN'T is the word that stops my mind and brain from working then I need to give it a jump start after saying the word. For me I will immediately start to think about what I can do. I begin to think of who would be a good person to help me get this turned around, or what books I can read that show the task being done or how to do it. It is when you start thinking about it differently that the wheels start to turn in your mind and you begin to feel a sense of pleasure and excitement. You begin offering LIFE happy feelings. This process won't be easy and it will be especially hard if you are accustomed to giving up on your dreams and ideas.

Isn't it amazing how one minute we can be happy and the next minute we can be sad? You have probably heard people say that in order to get over something, you must first face and deal with what's going on inside you. It is when we begin to acknowledge or deal with something that we begin to change our moods, feelings and attitude towards it.

I watched my best friend, who passed away of cancer, experience this. The best times he had were when he knew he could and would beat this disease. He was strong and knew he would be okay. It wasn't until his doctors told him the chemotherapy wasn't working anymore that he began to believe he was no longer able to win his fight. He began to feel as though he couldn't go on anymore and soon after, he lost his battle with cancer. Doctors at the beginning of diagnosing many cancer patients will tell them to change their diets and begin taking better care of themselves. More importantly to keep a good attitude, because doctors know your attitude can help you through anything. Doctors tell stories of patients diagnosed with a short amount of time to live, who live for years because of their attitude. What are you going to do to change your attitude about something negative happening in your life?

LIFE TIP: The word CAN'T gives your brain permission to stop trying.

4

Everyone is Not Your Friend

Do you have a person or job that isn't productive in your life anymore? Do they continue to add unwanted stress to your life? If so, you need to start putting together a game plan to make changes in your LIFE immediately. The moment you find something you don't like in any area of your LIFE you need to make changes. It may start out small, but it will ultimately blow up into something huge, and when LIFE does its random checking of your mood, feelings and attitude what will it find? An unhappy person, who is ready to have an unhappy day. You have a few good days, but the moment someone says something contrary to how you are feeling you immediately get an attitude. Isn't it amazing how we can get out of bed at 7 in the morning in a good mood and by

8:30 a.m. all hell can break lose? What happened in that time? Maybe you stubbed your toe getting out of bed, the iron leaked on your clothes, the hot water was all gone, you're out of milk, you can't find your keys and while you were rushing so you wouldn't be late, you spilled coffee on your clothes. When things are going bad is the time we must regroup, laugh and understand that the only thing we can control in situations like these is our reaction to what's going on. We won't be able to control the action that has taken place, because it's already in the past, and on page 43 we will learn that our "Point of Power is in the Present."

Things will happen, that's LIFE, but it is how we respond to LIFE that is the key. Once we stub our toe and feel the pain; we don't go over to the bed and do it again. When we taste something we don't like, we don't continue to eat it. With certain things we make changes to our actions immediately, with other things such as jobs or relationships we hang in there even though it may not be healthy for us. With certain things we take care of ourselves, and with other things we somehow feel like it's a badge of honor to keep taking the hits.

You shouldn't give up the moment things aren't going right. But if anything in your LIFE is constantly causing you to have a bad attitude, you need to evaluate what needs to be changed. When LIFE is checking, you want to be ready for it with a fantastic attitude to receive some extraordinary results.

Some people may say that even if they change the things around them, they can't get rid of all the negative people in their life. They don't have to, but they must change the relationship they have with them. You don't have to fellowship or hang out with everyone, and you shouldn't want to. Try to remember that everyone isn't running the same race, and everyone is not going to the same place. If you continue to run the race of others you may end up at their destination and not yours.

LIFE TIP: Unhealthy relationships and thoughts can be just as deadly as cancer, diabetes or any other life threatening illness if not treated.

CAN

5

Focus on Your Desires and Dreams

Whatever you do the most, whether that is complaining or celebrating, you will become good at it. Whatever you focus on, or give the most attention to, you will get more of it. That's' LIFE. LIFE will continue to give you more of what you focus your attention on. Whether negative or positive, LIFE is obedient to your wants and needs. If you dream of things, and will do anything to get it, LIFE will help you figure out ways to achieve your dreams. LIFE will even place people around you who think like you. My pastor travels around the world preaching and singing about Jesus Christ. He has won numerous awards and has a travel schedule that is very hectic. When I first met him it had been my dream to travel around the world speaking about leadership, motivation and the power of education. How did I find myself coming in contact with someone who is doing exactly what I want to do? The message is different, but the results are similar.

LIFE TIP: LIFE will put people around you with inspirations, dreams and desires similar to yours.

6

The Point of Power is in the Present

"The Point of Power is in the Present" means right now you are most powerful and your past doesn't dictate your future. Commit to saying "The Point of Power is in the Present" for 21 straight days. The moment you feel stressed, angry or confused, say it. You lost your job, your car won't start, your partner just broke up with you...what will you do right now, in this very moment when you are most powerful? How will your attitude be? What will your mood be like? How will you feel? Remember, LIFE is always checking. When you go from feeling bad for yourself to good about your options is when you will begin to have different results in your LIFE. When you start thinking about what you would like, instead of what you wouldn't like, your mood, feelings and attitude about things begin to change.

The moment you start examining your LIFE is the moment the results you have been receiving from LIFE can change. We all want control over our LIFE, which is a fine and noble concept, but we must also understand we have to exist with others. Can we control them? No, so to really take control over your LIFE, you must first realize that the only thing that you can control is how you react to others and to things that happen around you. You control your mood, feelings and attitude. LIFE is happening, whether you want it to or not, whether you're happy or whether you're sad, it's happening.

We must tap into LIFE more intentionally. This will be a process; first you have to decide what you want. I mean what you really want outside of that limiting box we continue to place ourselves in. This will be difficult to do at first because we are used to thinking about the things we don't want. When helping my student-athletes choose classes, I start by asking them what classes they want to take. Their responses may be, "I don't want any hard classes." This happens with my wife as well. We go to a restaurant and I ask her what she is thinking about having for dinner. Her response is usually, "I don't want anything with too many carbs." We are good at saying what we don't want, but we need to begin focusing a little more on what we do want.

We must also be more deliberate about taking care of ourselves. We need to be okay with self preservation and not feel guilty about it. In order to help others we must take care of ourself. In one of his songs, rapper Jay Z says, "I can't help the poor if I'm one of them, so I get rich and give back; to me that's the win win."

LIFE TIP: You must feed your mind with good thoughts, the same way you feed your body with good food.

INNER POWER

7

Importance of Haters

During my presentations to young men and women I ask them to pretend I am Mr. Webster of Webster dictionary. Every year words are added to the dictionary, and this year we have selected the word HATER. What I'm looking for is a definition for this word that is commonly used throughout different communities. I ask them for their definition of the word:

- Anyone who is jealous of what you have or what you can do.
- Anyone who talks about you behind your back.
- Anyone who doesn't have your best interest in mind.

I agree with every statement. Next I ask if having a HATER in their LIFE is a good or a bad thing, and most of them will say it is a bad thing. I believe having a HATER or

HATERS in your LIFE can be a great thing. Then I give them my definition:

> A HATER is a person who is unhappy with the direction their LIFE is headed, or someone who has allowed CAN'T to become one of their most commonly used words. They want this to become your reality as well.

I believe HATERS play a necessary and vital role in your LIFE, a role that can help you dream bigger than you ever thought possible.

If a HATER is constantly telling you what you CAN'T do, because they couldn't, you should want to figure out a way to make it happen just because they said that it could not happen. Most haters are unhappy about the direction their life is headed, so use their life as a blueprint of what not to do, as well as look at the source that is speaking these negative things to you.

- HATERS should help you stimulate decisions and desires for action in your LIFE.
- HATERS should make you want to do it just to show them it is possible.
- Use HATERS to make you want to change different areas in your LIFE.

Here are some steps to defeating the HATERS in your life, steps that will help you to live your dreams.

Step 1 — Determine what you want.

This may seem easy but it may be one of the most difficult steps due to our tendency to focus on what can't happen. We have to step out of that make believe box of limitations we place ourselves in and believe in the impossible. We can't allow our situation to determine our destination. If you change the way you view yourself in spite of the situation, LIFE will bend your race to a new destination. It is amazing how this works; and it happens all the time when we believe. This has happened for numerous people. Famous NBA player Mugsy Bogues was only 5'3", can you imagine what his high school counselors may have told him when he said he wanted to play in the NBA. Jim Abbott was born without a right hand. I can imagine what his high school counselors may have said when he told them he wanted to play major league baseball. LIFE is working for everyone, every second, minute, hour to bend to their mood, feeling and attitude.

I have had young ladies who come into my office in tears, crying about how bad their reputation was, and I offer these words of advice, "Change the way YOU view yourself regardless of how others view you." At first this is difficult for them to hear, but I tell them it's really simple when you begin to practice. When you begin to work on you and begin to define yourself without any help from others, you can create the person you want to become. The student had allowed others to define who they thought she should become and in doing so, she had given others the power to affect her happiness. We should never allow this power to be given to anyone. This power is the fire that will ignite us to become great. I tell my clients that it is crucial to start defining who they would like to be without help from others. We have all made mistakes and bad decisions, and LIFE knows it, but LIFE isn't keeping score.

The score card is clean, the slate is at zero and every hour, minute, second; we determine the direction of the race. Change can happen immediately, if we throw away our score cards. The choice is up to us on how long we want to stay in a bad relationship or feel bad about the many mistakes we all make. We cannot continue to allow one area of our LIFE to affect all areas of our LIFE.

In determining what you want, you need to begin building a list of things you would like to have or achieve. One of my partners and I travel around the country presenting seminars on goal setting. During these presentations we bring a large variety of magazines and pictures. Toward the end of the seminar we have our clients use these magazines to select pictures to create a dream board. We all have some things we would like to do or places we would like to visit. Dream boards help us visualize all of the things we desire. In these presentations we want them to conceptualize what they visualize to help them materialize. We ask our clients to find a place in their home where they can look at their dream board for at least one minute a day, everyday. We want them to begin focusing and giving attention to their dreams and desires.

When you begin to focus on the things in your LIFE you want and begin to turn your concentration from the things you don't have, your mood, feeling and attitude will change. This is when you will start to see different things happening around you and in your LIFE.

Imagine for a moment you have this great power inside you that is willing to help you bend and shape things to your heart's desires. How would you use it? Would you take advantage of people? Would you help people? However you choose to use it will determine how successful you can become. Remember LIFE is always checking on us to see what we are up to, and when it's checking we want to make sure we are doing things that will help our mood, feelings and attitude, because our emotions will affect what we receive.

Step 2 — Focus on the things you would like.

Think about this power I just spoke of and imagine it is inside you but is very weak. Imagine it being out of shape, malnourished, and suffering from lack of usage. Every now and then it rises up to give you some of those things you have wanted, or helped you make a better decision about a choice you were going to make. But because it was so weak you didn't notice what it was or what it was doing because you didn't see it or feel it that often.

We need to strengthen, feed, and nourish this power we have to make it work more diligently in our LIFE. This journey starts with our attitude. When you have a better attitude about doing things you don't feel like doing, and begin doing these things with joy, you will begin to see the benefits. You may have to stretch your mind to see the benefits from doing these things, but they do exist. An example is taking out your trash at home. This task is not one most people enjoy. Turn this experience around and be grateful you have the opportunity to have trash. It is a privilege to have all the items that contribute to the trash. Be thankful for the food you have to eat, the paper towels you were able to purchase, and all the other things that have accumulated. Once you realize this, you will begin to have joy about the simple task of taking out the trash.

It may be hard to see how working at McDonalds on the fry machine can benefit you unless you change your attitude. People who now own a McDonalds franchise may have started out working just like you, but they had a different attitude when working with the fries. They understood that learning every aspect of how McDonalds worked would allow them to understand what it would take to run the business. A lot of successful people used what they learned at jobs like this, that most would view as a dead end, and used that information and knowledge to help them get to where they are today.

They were able to feed that power in them with the knowledge they learned from cooking fries, to help them to accomplish their ultimate goal. Everyday LIFE teaches us something, but in many cases our inner power is too weak to accept it. You can start on the fry machine and end up wherever your mood, feelings or attitude takes you. Keep in mind LIFE is obedient and whatever you're focusing on, LIFE will bring it to you. If your focus is solely on fries, then you will be the best fry maker in the McDonalds franchise.

You have to ask yourself what you want and what you hope to become at this time in your LIFE. Do you want to feed and nourish that inner power or continue to ignore your desires, hopes and dreams?

Your inner power will be weak initially. For any of you who are getting back in shape, were you able to take all that weight off, that took years to put on, after one day of working out? Were you back in shape instantly or did you have to stick with it? For many of us we have never consciously used this inner power, so it will take time to get it back in shape. Trainers and health advisors will tell you that we should all be walking or doing some sort of exercise once a day for at least 30 minutes. This applies to using inner power as well. We should be taking time out at least once a day for a few moments, because any work you do to strengthen your inner power will ultimately make it stronger.

You have to begin using this power to pull positive people and things closer to you. You also have to begin to celebrate those positive things that happen to you, because LIFE will see you celebrating and begin to give you more of what you are celebrating about. The same is true for what you are negative about; LIFE will bring you more negativity if that is what you are celebrating or dwelling on. When LIFE is checking to see what your mood, feeling, or attitude is, you want to be working on or using your inner power. Whether it's for one minute or 30 minutes, you want to be working on your inner power so it can give you more of what you are focusing on. During that time you don't want to be offering worry, anger, frustration or anything that doesn't build your inner power. Remember, you have been good at offering a negative disposition for a long time, and receiving what LIFE has been giving you. This is about changing our thoughts, moods, feeling and attitude to receive different outcomes.

"How long will this process take," people often ask me.

I respond by asking them, "how often will you utilize the power within you?"

When things are going bad, and people are being negative around you, what will your mood be? Will you revert back to having a negative mood, feeling or attitude? Or will you take a moment and use the power within you to help think of different ways your LIFE could change if you change? You must stop doubting. There is always a way out of every situation, if you allow your inner power to lead you.

When you begin to understand how powerful this inner power is, and begin to utilize it, is when you will begin to see things change in your LIFE. Utilizing this power is the key to your success. This power is what we all must utilize in order to be successful. One of the things that separates successful people from others is their ability to tap into this power. Successful people have a short memory, they tend to not wallow in what happened to them for too long; they shake it off, make changes and move to the next thing they want to achieve.

Some people may say this will be hard for them. When you were a child, walking may have been hard until you practiced. Eating solid food also took some time, and learning your ABC's may have seemed like something you just picked up. But trust me, "L-ah MO P" was not part of it. You had to learn after practicing many times, that it was L, M, N, O and then P!

Once you start to give your hopes, desires, and dreams your focus and attention, you will begin to watch things manifest around you and in your LIFE. The moment you start to focus on your dreams and desires, a little voice may begin to tell you what you CAN'T do and what you CAN'T have. It may try to convince you that you are not worthy of having good things happen to you.

This voice may try to cancel out your positive mood, feelings or attitude. I'm not a math major, but I was taught early on that any number multiplied by zero is zero. The same is true for our dreams and desires when we allow doubt to come in. Any dream multiplied by doubt will cancel out our desire and leave us with zero. So you must remove the doubt from the equation.

What have you been giving your attention to? And whatever your answer is, do you have a lot of it? Earlier I spoke about having a bad day, and it usually will start out that way and get worse and worse. This is because we gave our attention to it. We had no doubt our day would be bad when that coffee first spilled on us or when that person cut us off when we were driving. This is power working inside of us making LIFE bend to the way we want it to be. So whatever you are receiving in your LIFE is a result of how much doubt you allowed to come in to receive it. If you didn't allow doubt to come in and overpower your dreams you would receive them.

Again- step-one is to define what your desires are, and be specific. If it is a red car, what kind, what year, make and model, only you can decide if you will be just as happy with a orange 1966 Chrysler or a 2009 Cadillac Escalade.

Step-two is to focus on your desires, create a dream board, cut out pictures of things you desire and then post this board where you can see it often.

Do you ever wonder how people around you continue to accumulate certain things? Why them and why not me? I will guarantee they have been focusing on it, and you may have even heard them bragging about it. Think about that friend of yours who always has a different companion, what it is they talk about all the time? What about your other friends who are always broke and never have any money, what are the words that come out of their mouth? I'm sure they don't doubt they will be broke, just as the other doesn't doubt they will have a companion. It's the absence of doubt that allows us to achieve our dreams and desires.

You must learn how to eliminate doubt from your mind when it comes to things you want. You should stop placing limits on what your inner power can do and help you to become.

If Michael Jordan is arguably one of the greatest players to ever play the game of basketball, then why did he get cut from his junior varsity basketball team? I wonder if there was a time in his life where he had to tap in and use this inner power to work harder than anyone else. I wonder if he changed his actions to believe he could become great and while doing this, LIFE was checking his mood and feelings and brought his dreams and desires to pass.

What do you tell yourself you can do or what you can become? What do you think about constantly? What are the limits you place on yourself? The answers to these questions will determine if LIFE will allow you too achieve your dreams and desires. You have to begin to ask LIFE for what you want, and believe without a doubt you will receive it. Since LIFE isn't keeping score of what you did in the past, and because LIFE is checking every hour, minute and second, you must believe you are worthy of receiving your dreams and desires. As soon as you begin to remove any doubt of obtaining these things, you will.

If everyone has the same inner workings and it's only our outside exterior that is different, that would lead me to believe the only difference between people would be the way they live LIFE and utilize their individual inner power. If other people can do it, or have it, why can't you? Once you start seeing things changing in your life, and people starting to act different around you...celebrate it.

My wife always gets a chuckle whenever we go to the store, because I always get a parking space in the front. I don't think it was anything I did, besides believing that I could. No one called my house from the store we were going to and informed me they were leaving at 10:30. What happens is every time I leave the house, I know I will get a great parking spot. I have no doubt whatsoever, I also understand that someone who was in the store earlier will be coming out soon if I am patient. I never know when, I just know it will be soon. I have patience and believe without doubt that this will always happen.

This is small and may seem insignificant to some, but this is where and how it may start for you. When I pull into that parking space I feel like I just kicked the winning field goal in a super bowl game, because I know LIFE is checking every hour, minute and second and I want my mood, feelings and attitude to be in line when it's checking. It all goes back to what you believe in, and whatever it is you must celebrate it, no matter how big or small.

You have to begin to train your mind to ask for things you want, and believe you can have them. You must remove any doubt and start believing you can have the desires of your heart. Remember, if others are doing it or having it, why not you? If you have to talk yourself into it, then do just that.

I enjoy watching MTV Cribs for this very reason. I believe if others can live like that so can I. My wife would ask how I could watch the same episodes of Cribs again and again. She doesn't ask anymore because she now understands and believes I'm getting design ideas for our next home. My wife watches how I bend LIFE to work with me and for me, and she believes. Early in our relationship, I would tell her what I was going to do and who I was going to become. Now I say it one time and she watches it happen. It doesn't happen overnight, but I have no doubt it will happen, no matter how long it takes.

Now I surround myself with people who have a similar belief system, and whose moods, feelings and attitudes are balanced. I have a network of people who help me stretch beyond my limitations.

These people, unlike the HATER, will help build you. They will allow you to enjoy your new direction, and talk about all the wonderful things LIFE is doing for you. The HATER will drain LIFE out of you and make you feel uncomfortable about saying things around them because they will feel jealous.

LIFE TIP: Any dream multiplied by doubt will cancel out your desire and leave you with zero.

TAKE ACTION

8

Take Action, Find Your Passion

I always knew there was something different about me, and that I would be successful. One night while in college I took a break from working on my thesis for my first Master's degree. I decided to take a drive and there was a party on this particular street that I drove down. The reason I wasn't at this party was because I knew that in order to have things others didn't, I had to be willing to do things others wouldn't. As I was driving by I saw a good friend and quickly made a u-turn to say hi.

I had no intentions of staying at the party; I just wanted to say hi to my friend. I parked, got out of my car and everyone said hi and mentioned how nice my car was. They were all acting extremely friendly towards me and this began to annoy my friend. He pulled me to the side and told me these same guys were saying bad things about me before I arrived. I thanked him for telling me, and told him not to worry about it.

The next day he called me, "How were you so cool? Why didn't you get upset?" I laughed and explained to him that I knew because I had decided to quit hanging out and began doing things different, they would feel like I wasn't one of them anymore. I was okay with this; I understood that in order to be them, I would have to continue to lose me. Once my mood, feelings and attitude begin to change, I began to like me and who I was becoming.

I won't say it was easy training my mind to think like this, but I will say my doubt did not outweigh what I was feeling at this particular time in my life. I was determined to be successful and unwilling to let anyone or anything interfere with this. I knew if I kept my mood, feelings and attitude in check, I would be okay. Your mission can't be to have everyone like you, it will never happen. Remember you can only change you and your reaction.

This process becomes much easier when you have others around who believe without a doubt that your dreams can happen. Get around someone who you can sharpen and who can sharpen you. Try to stay away from that person or those people who bring you down, and are doing the very same thing you would like to change about yourself. At the beginning it will be easier for them to pull you towards something that is not good for you until you strengthen your inner power. So until you work on your mood, feelings and attitude, you may find yourself dropping down to a level that won't help you grow.

I tell my students all the time that I grow, when we grow, so when my students come in my office feeling down or angry with someone, I always try to find the words that will help strengthen their inner power.

They may come to my office feeling sad over a grade they received on a test and I ask them how much time they put into studying. More often than not, it wasn't what it should have been. "Now that this test is over and you can't go back and take it again, what will you do to prepare for the next test in order to avoid receiving these unwanted results?" I ask. Most say, as I hoped they would, they intend to study more, and will expect to receive different results. Albert Einstein said the definition of insanity is continuing to do the same thing, and expecting different results.

I have friends who call me complaining about their job and I ask them what they are doing in order to make an easy transition to leave the place causing their mood, feelings and attitude to negatively affect their LIFE in this way. I won't allow them to have a pity party for themselves, and I won't feed their negative way of thinking. I'm always cautious when it comes to offering advice about their job, because I know many of them can't just up and leave their only source of income.

What I do is offer them options. I remind them about technology and how they can earn a degree online at universities that cater to the older adult with busy schedules. If you begin working on learning something that will increase your knowledge, you will place yourself in a position where you have options to leave that job causing you so much anguish.

It won't be easy, and it may seem like every road block will come up against you. This will continue to happen until you strengthen that inner power and allow it to start working with you. Most importantly you must understand that someone somewhere was in a similar position at one time. They were unhappy with their job; they took steps to change their situation, and now love what they are doing. If you are unhappy with your circumstances, how hard are you willing to work to change them? Once you begin this process of change to strengthen that inner power, you will find things begin to change in your LIFE. Positive things will begin to gravitate towards you, all because when LIFE was checking, it found your mood, feelings and attitude in alignment and because it's obedient, it will continue to give you more of this feeling. Be warned, some of your friends, some people who you associate with, will get mad at you for always wanting to make them get better by evaluating their LIFE, and they will stop coming around you.

This is okay because you are moving to another level in your LIFE and they are taking a different path. You have to draw a line in the sand of how you would like to be treated, and what you expect from the people around you. Understand that if that line is crossed, you're entitled to make changes in your LIFE that may not include them.

You, and only you, can decide how you would like to be treated and what you are willing to put up with. If you no longer choose to listen to gossip, trust me they will find someone else who will. If you don't choose to act in an unethical way, they will find someone who will. You can find and do what you want, if you continue to have a positive mood, feeling and attitude.

Hopefully, this book has helped you to see that "It's not a Secret, it's just LIFE" and your mood, feelings and attitude towards LIFE will determine if you can achieve your dreams and desires. These lessons are already in you, and it is my goal to help ordinary people realize they have the ability to do extraordinary things. Remember, every great journey started with a footstep. Keep imagining and dreaming, and continue to break chains. If you keep taking shots at the moon, don't worry if you miss; you can still land among the stars.

LIFE TIP: Finding your passion will take action and in order to have things others don't, you have to be willing to do things others won't.

To order copies, contact:

Dr. D.F. Arnold
1139 Grand Bluffs Dr. SW
Grand Rapids, MI 49534
Phone: (616) 482-9291
E-mail: lead@dfarnold.com
Website: www.dfarnold.com

CPSIA information can be obtained at www.ICGtesting.com
Printed in the USA
BVOW06s1953190216

437028BV00007B/6/P

9 781589 096189